TABLE OF CONTENTS

INTRODUCTION

"Gentlemen - We just lost the initiative" [1]

- Major General William F. Garrison

The Region

In Somalia in 1993, famine and civil war riddled the country resulting in hundreds of thousands of civilian deaths leading to a major United Nations (U.N.) peacekeeping operation. With most of the peacekeepers withdrawn, the Somali militia declared war on the remaining U.N. personnel. In response, America's elite soldiers: the Army Rangers, Delta Force and the Special Operations Aviation Regiment – named Task Force Ranger, deployed to Somalia under the command of Major General William F. Garrison in support of Operation Restore Hope.[2] Following significant U.S. causalities during the Battle of Mogadishu, the mission culminated in a strategic disaster for the United States scarring U.S. public opinion and policy on Somalia. To this day, Somalia remains a politically sensitive and emotive issue impacting U.S. policy not only in Somalia, but also the Horn of Africa (HOA) region. The instability and lack of a formal government in Somalia has created ideal conditions for an Al Qaeda (AQ) safe haven.

---

[1] Quotes from the Movie *"Blackhawk Down,"* First Quotes, Major General William Garrison, Commander, Task Force Ranger.
http://www.finestquotes.com/movie_quotes/movie/Black%20Hawk%20Down/page/0.htm (accessed February 5, 2012).

[2] Ray Snyder, *Operation Restore Hope/Battle of Mogadishu*, History 135, August 2001, http://novaonline.nvcc.edu/eli/evans/his135/Events/Somalia93/Somalia93.html (accessed August 3, 2011).

Thesis

This thesis will identify the clear and present danger that Somalia's terrorist and violent extremist networks (VEN) pose to our country and if U.S. policy remains unchanged will lead to attacks within our borders. In the interest of our homeland security, Somalia cannot continue to serve as a safe haven for terrorists. This thesis will identify the issue our country faces and provide recommendations to mitigate the Somalia terrorist threat. Additionally, this thesis will make recommendations that provide military and diplomatic measures that could be implemented in order to reduce the risk of attacks within the borders of our homeland emanating from Somalia.

Background

Somalia aptly defines the term anarchy and the Muslim nation has been without an effective government for over two decades and continues to be the most –failed of failed states on the continent" creating the perfect safe haven for terrorist activity. [3] Al Qaeda's role in international terrorism poses a threat to our homeland more so now than anytime following the World Trade Center attack on 9-11. Due to the military successes in Afghanistan and Iraq, Al Qaeda is moving abroad to countries such as Somalia that offer them safe haven and allow them to continue training and planning attacks on the United States, its interests, and its allies. Currently Somalia with its ties to the diasporas, the large ethnic Somali population of U.S. citizens who reside within our

---

[3] Jane's Terrorism and Insurgency Center, Somalia: Forgotton Terrorism Base, February 33, 2005. http://jtic.janes.com (accessed October 15, 2011).

country's major cities, poses a significant internal threat. Current U.S. policy does not address this threat.

Al Qaeda's ability to launch large scale attacks has been diminished; however the group is taking advantage of a weak central government in Somalia that exercises little or no control over its vast region. The ability of Al Qaeda to extend its reach beyond its core members is growing daily and it is important to understand the nature of this evolving danger. Despite Al Qaeda's organizational leadership transformation in Somalia, its strategic objectives remain the same: to attack the United States and governments seen supporting the United States.

U.S. policy makers understand the growing strategic importance of Africa, particularly the mounting concern over violent extremist activities. On February 6, 2007, the Bush Administration announced the creation of a new unified combatant command, U.S. Africa Command (AFRICOM) to promote U.S. national security objectives in the region. As outlined in its charter, Africa Command is tasked to —protect U.S. interests" in the region through military operations if directed by the National Command Authority. [4] As U.S. Africa Command continues to refine its Theater Campaign Plan, results of this analysis will identify planning priority shortfalls and offer specific recommendations for both operational and theater strategic objectives. The lack of emphasis on Somalia as a terrorist safe haven permeates U.S. Africa Command's theater campaign strategy that has geographic responsibility for Somalia.

---

[4] Lauren Ploch, Africa Command: U.S. Strategic Interests and the Role of the U.S. Military in Africa, Congressional Research Service - RL34003, July 22, 2011, 5.

Overview of Remaining Chapters

The enemy is migrating to a transnational movement of extremist organizations, networks, and individuals and this movement to countries that offer a safe haven is the most dangerous manifestation of this threat. This thesis will assess the current homeland security threat emanating from Somalia. Chapter 1 provides an overview of the recent developments in Somalia as well as the critical actors involved which include Somalia's Transitional Federal Government (TFG), the African Union Mission in Somalia (AMISOM), and the Al Shabaab terrorist Network. Additionally, this chapter discusses the aspects of a safe haven and how Somalia's lack of governance created the ideal conditions for the Al Shabaab terrorist network to establish their control in the region. Chapter 2 builds on the atmospherics in Somalia and ties the threats to our homeland by analyzing the Somalia diaspora in our major cities citing specific examples and trends that have occurred and that presently exist. This chapter will also focus on the recruitment and radicalization of U.S. citizens and highlight the threat they present in our country. Chapter 3 will detail the existence of the Al Shabaab training camps that exist in Somalia, focusing on how they were created and why they are successful in recruiting U.S. citizens and how individuals who trained in these camps have executed terrorist attacks abroad. Chapter 4 will address the current U.S. policy on Somalia focusing on identification of the threat and current policy shortfalls at the strategic level of government in the National Security Strategy and the U.S. Defense strategies. Finally, Chapter 5 will further identify issues at the operational and tactical level at Africa Command (AFRICOM), the geographic Combatant Command that has oversight of

Somalia, and its ability to develop an overarching strategy and supporting plans to disrupt the terrorist threat in Somalia.

CHAPTER 1: OVERVIEW OF THE CURRENT ENVIRONMENT

"If ignorant both of your enemy and yourself, you are certain to be in peril" [1]

— Sun Tzu

Situation

This chapter will provide an overview of the current situation, as well as the major events that lead up to the current crisis in Somalia that has created the safe haven that currently exists. Since 9-11, Al Qaeda has transformed and evolved into a different organization than the terrorist cell that planned and executed the attacks on the World Trade Center over a decade ago. In 1995, the Department of Defense highlighted its view of Africa in its U.S. Security Strategy on Africa stating that ―ultimately we see very little strategic interest in Africa.‖[2] This theme continues to prevail. In order to understand the current crisis in Somalia, it is important to understand past events in Somali governance by the Transnational Federal Government (TFG), African Union Mission in Somalia (AMISOM), and the impact of Al-Shabaab.

As noted by Charlie Szrom from the American Enterprise Institute, ―The environment in which an Al Qaeda affiliate operates is one of the most important factors

---

[1] Sun Tsu, *The Art of War*, Popular Quotes, http://www.artofwar net/china/quotes htm (accessed February 5, 2012).

[2] U.S. Department of Defense, Office of the Assistant Secretary of Defense (Public Affairs) Speech on U.S. Security Strategy for Sub-Saharan Africa, Published by the Office of International Security Affairs, Department of Defense, August 01, 1995. 2.

in assessing the threat it poses to U.S. interests."[3] In his report he goes on to state that the environment —determines the group's strength, capabilities, and character more than any other single factor. Denying Al Qaeda and its affiliate's access to environments propitious to their operations can significantly reduce the terror threat to the United States."[4]

Transitional Federal Government

The Transitional Federal Government (TFG) is the internationally recognized government of the Republic of Somalia backed by the United Nations, the African Union as well as the United States. The TFG was formed in late 2004 and was initially located in Kenya until June 2005. Parliament did not convene inside Somalia borders until February 2006 in the western city of Baidoa because security concerns kept the legislature from entering Mogadishu. After convening, the TFG lacked cohesion which undermined its power. In July 2007, after months of delay, the TFG convened a reconciliation conference where key parties, including moderate Islamists, chose to boycott instead of attending. Due to this boycott, many experts deemed the conference a failure.[5] The TFG under the leadership of President Yusuf —was weak, ineffective, and seriously debilitated by defections" and in 2008-2009, an estimated 40% of the police

---

[3] Charlie Szrom, *Al Qaeda's Operating Environment – A New Approach to the War on Terror*, American Enterprise Institute, March 2011.

[4] Ibid, 1.

[5] AMISOM: African Mission in Somalia, The African Union Commission, 2008, http://www.africa-union.org/root/au/auc/departments/psc/amisom/amisom_htm, (accessed September 13, 2011).

force, trained by the United Nations, left the force due to lack of payment.[6] The TFG currently governs from southern Mogadishu, where the security situation remains dire.

African Union Mission in Somalia

As Somalia continued to suffer, the African Union created the African Union Mission in Somalia (AMISOM) in the 69th Communiqué of the African Union Peace and Security Council which was ratified on January 19, 2007. During this African Union Summit the countries of Ghana, Nigeria, Burundi and Malawi pledged to provide troops, but as of February 2010, only about 5,300 AMISOM troops were present, located mostly in strategic locations in the capital, Mogadishu. Only Uganda and Burundi have actually contributed troops to AMISOM and the mandate calls for 8,000.[7] Although many other African Union countries pledged to provide troops, none except Uganda and Burundi have done so.

The mission of AMISOM was to conduct Peace Support Operations in Somalia, stabilize the security situation including the take over from Ethiopian Forces and to create a safe and secure environment in preparation for the transition to the U.N.[8] In concept, this mission worked well initially. However, the situation in Somalia was beyond the scope and capability for AMISOM to control, primarily due to the inability of both AMISOM and the TFG to fight an insurgency against an Islamic organization named Al-

---

[6] Ted Dagne, *Somalia: Current Conditions and Prospects for a Lasting Peace*, Specialist in African Affairs, Congressional Research Service, August 31, 2011, 13.

[7] AMISOM: African Mission in Somalia, The African Union Commission, 2008, http://www.africa-union.org/root/au/auc/departments/psc/amisom/amisom htm, (accessed September 13, 2011).

[8] Ibid.

Shabaab. —The military units trained in neighboring countries for the TFG are disintegrating because of a lack of maintenance and leadership. Most of them joined Al Shabaab as an already trained fighting force."[9]

Al Shabaab

Al Shabaab, Al Qaeda's major ally in East Africa, is an Islamic organization that controls much of southern Somalia, excluding the capital city of Mogadishu. It has waged an insurgency against Somalia's transitional government and its Ethiopian supporters since 2006.[10] Senior Somali officials, African Union sources, and other regional officials estimate that more than –400 foreign fighters from Afghanistan, Yemen, Pakistan, the United States, Canada, United Kingdom, Kenya, and Saudi Arabia have been engaged in support of the Al Shabaab forces."[11]

The current humanitarian situation in Somalia peaked in 2009 following new fighting in Mogadishu between the TFG and Al Shabaab. Somalis left their homes and communities because of the dangers of conflict but also because they had become direct targets of violence. Those working with the TFG received death threats from extremist groups. Because the Somali government was non-functional and regional security mechanisms remained weak, displacement and criminal activities were carried out in an

---

[9] Somalia: Current Situation, Somaliweyn, December 31, 2010, http://somaliweyn.somaliweyn.org/index.php?Itemid=9&catid=3:english-news&id=261:somalia-current-situation&option=com_content&view=article (accessed September 1, 2011).

[10] Stephanie Hanson, *Al-Shabaab*, Council on Foreign Relations, August 10, 2011, http://www.cfr.org/somalia/al-shabaab/p18650 (accessed September 13, 2011).

[11] Dagne, 13.

environment of impunity due to the lack of the rule of law in Somalia. Al Shabaab declared the United Nations (U.N.) personnel (including the humanitarian agencies) to be a legitimate military target because the U.N. was training the TFG's police forces. This was interesting in light of the hypothesis that extremist groups would not want to be seen as the direct cause for the suffering of the Somali people. But if agencies like the U.N. are seen as aiding their enemies, extremist groups see these agencies as their enemies as well.[12]

On 5 February 2010, Somali Al Shabaab extremists announced that they were forming an alliance with Al Qaeda to establish an Islamic state in Somalia and fight a *jihad* across East Africa. This statement crystallizes what is at stake in a country that has been ripped apart by war for two decades.[13]

As of December 30, 2010 the country was for the most part under Al Shabaab rule. Al Shabaab continued a sustained military offensive against the TFG and AMISOM. The main artery road (Maka Al Mukarama) linking Aden Abdulle Osman International Airport and Villa Somalia served as a battle zone. There are two substantial elements that significantly compound this complex situation. First, the TFG had neither the necessary financial means nor the military force to defeat Al Shabaab, while AMISOM did not have the mandate to engage Al Shabaab outside of its garrisons in Mogadishu. Secondly, paradoxically, the U.N. arms embargo on Somalia prohibits

---

[12] The changing Security Situation in Somalia: Implications for Humanitarian Action, The Brookings Institution, January 12, 2010, http://www.brookings.edu/~/media/Files/events/2010/0112_somalia/0112_somalia.pdf (accessed August 28, 2011).

[13] AMISOM Bulletin, *Somalia is the Frontline in the Global Fight against Violent Extremism*, Issue 2, March 15, 2010, http://www.africa-union.org/root/au/auc/departments/psc/amisom/Bulletin/2010/AMISOM_%20BULLETIN_ISSUE%20NO%202.pdf (accessed September 13, 2011).

arming of any Somali entity. The winners of the arms embargo were those who did not abide by it, namely Al Shabaab and its associates.[14] What security forces were available were no match for the guerilla and suicide tactics of the Al Qaeda trained and re-enforced Al Shabaab fighters.

Al Shabaab, who has pledged loyalty to both Al Qaeda and Al Qaeda in the Arabian Peninsula (AQAP), has the intent and capability to either attack or support an attack against the United States interests or the U.S. homeland. The United States appears to be high on Al Shabaab's list of international targets. The group began issuing threats against the United States and it professes an ideology resembling AQ's. It has pledged allegiance to the late Bin Laden and views itself as fighting the global *jihad* led by AQ.[15]

Somalia – a Safe Haven

On January 21, 2010 Senator John Kerry, the Chairman of the United States Foreign Relations Committee stated that the changing nature of Al Qaeda poses a greater threat to the U.S. homeland now more that ever due to the hundreds or even thousands of fighters that have traveled to regions that offer a safe haven to continue planning and preparing for attacks. In his report, he literally calls this movement of foreign fighters a ―ticking time bomb" implying that it is only a matter of time before the United States

---

[14] Somalia: Current Situation, Somaliweyn, December 31, 2010, http://somaliweyn.somaliweyn.org/index.php?Itemid=9&catid=3:english-news&id=261:somalia-current-situation&option=com_content&view=article (accessed September 1, 2011).

[15] Christopher Harnisch, *The Terror Threat from Somalia: The internationalization of Al Shabaab*, American Enterprise Institute, February 12, 2010.1.

suffers another attack within our borders.[16] Al Qaeda recruitment now focuses on

American citizens to carry out their attack which is a drastic change in tactics.

It is important to understand the environment in Somalia to grasp the threat our

country faces in order to explain the context of why terrorists are migrating to this region.

T.E. Lawrence (Lawrence of Arabia) recognized the need for a safe haven during the

Arab revolt against the Turks in 1916-1918.[17] He discusses the importance of a safe

haven in which to operate and how this is tied to the operational level of war; however,

Dr. Mackubin Owens, Professor of National Security Affairs at the Naval War College

states that the importance of the terrorist safe haven applies to all levels including

strategic and tactical. He added, ―understanding this fact permits us to recognize the

importance of the sanctuary as the cornerstone of the geopolitics of terrorism" and this is

the reason terrorists groups rely on the likes of Somalia.[18]

Al Qaeda in Iraq and Afghanistan are different from the Al Qaeda cells that are in

Somalia. The core Al Qaeda values still holds true – attack the U.S. and continue *jihad*,

however the networks in Somalia are governed by other factors not necessarily seen in

Iraq and Afghanistan. Michael E. Leiter, the Director of the National Counterterrorism

Center offered these remarks while at the Aspen Institute when asked about the

movement of Al Qaeda's center of gravity. ―I think what we see the greatest likelihood

of now is less centralized command and control, and no clear center of gravity." He

indicated that the focus of Al Qaeda's center of gravity can potentially move to an area

---

[16] Committee on Foreign Relations, *Al Qaeda in Yemen and Somalia: A ticking Time Bomb,* A Report to the Committee on Foreign Relations, 111th Congress, 2d Session, January 21, 2010. 4.

[17] T.E. Lawrence, *Revolt in the Desert* (New York. George H. Doran Company, 1926), 251.

[18] Jeffery H. Horwitz, *Pirate, Terrorists and Warloards* (New York: Skyhorse Publishing, 2009), 14.

like Somalia and have a greater effect.[19] ―Al Shabaab is increasing recruitment and training of fighters by the day. All the population centers (cities, towns, villages) in the south and central Somalia are effectively under Al Shabaab control. Estimates of several hundred to several thousand foreign fighters and experts from Al Qaeda and other radical groups enhance the ranks and the fighting quality of Al Shabaab."[20]

Al Qaeda Safe Havens in Afghanistan and Iraq

It is important to understand Al Qaeda's environmental and security requirements to grasp why Somalia benefits the terrorist groups. Before discussing why Somalia has been successful, we must first consider what has occurred before and after military operations in both Afghanistan and Iraq where Al Qaeda safe havens have been disrupted. For a terrorist group to be successful it must have leaders, planners, trainers, recruiters, funding, and propagandists. This ―network" is vast and developed over years and safe havens where terrorist groups have unencumbered freedom of maneuver are essential.

Al Qaeda could not have planned and executed the 9-11 attacks without the safe haven offered in Afghanistan. Al Qaeda used the Taliban in Afghanistan to provide both operating space and personnel, exactly what we see in Somalia by Al Shabaab. From within Afghanistan, Al Qaeda maintained a sustained terrorist campaign where they

---

[19] Remarks by Honorable Michael E. Leiter, Director National Counter Terrorism Center at the Aspen Institute, April 9, 2009, http://www.dni.gov/speeches/20090409_speech.pdf (accessed August 23, 2011).

[20] Somalia: Current Situation, Somaliweyn, December 31, 2010, http://somaliweyn.somaliweyn.org/index.php?Itemid=9&catid=3:english-news&id=261:somalia-current-situation&option=com_content&view=article (accessed September 1, 2011).

launched not one attack, but numerous successful mass casualty attacks on U.S. targets such as the American Embassies in East Africa, the USS *Cole* bombing and the 9-11 attack on the World Trade Center.

As the Taliban in Afghanistan was eliminated and major military operations continued to dismantle the terrorist network, we saw the migration of these groups. The diminishing environment in Afghanistan forced Al Qaeda to move into Pakistan where they capitalized on international policy between the U.S. and Pakistan that prevented the U.S. and coalition forces from targeting the terrorist cells. From there, Al Qaeda was able to continue attacks on U.S. and coalition forces. We also observed Al Qaeda attempt to move their operations to Iraq. Disrupting one operating environment does not mean that they can immediately reestablish themselves in another as we have seen in Pakistan. Al Qaeda's attempt to shift their ideology and leadership from Afghanistan to Iraq ultimately failed because U.S. forces partnered with the Iraqis and denied Al Qaeda time to develop an operational environment. Al Qaeda was unable to develop trust, relationships and the human networks to support itself. [21]   The safe haven hoped for by the Al Qaeda in Iraq ̶ proved too vulnerable and fragile for all the intensity and lethality the Al Qaeda network displayed there"[22] meaning that although Al Qaeda was initially successful in shifting operations from Afghanistan to Iraq, the coordinated efforts by the U.S. and the Iraqi militaries disrupted their efforts to gain and maintain a foothold for sustained and continuous attacks against coalition forces.

_____

[21] Szrom, 11.

[22] Ibid.

Why Somalia

There are three key characteristics that are common for terrorist safe havens: under-development, incompetent governance, and disillusioned citizenry; all of which exist in Somalia.[23] Terrorists groups may be able to operate without safe havens, but these areas significantly improve their ability to plan, train, recruit, equip and enhance their operational network. The most precious asset terror organizations have is their credibility in the eyes of their population and the support they expect to get based on this credibility.[24]

Somalia is plagued by a population with no hope, so it is important to consider the human dimension of terrorist groups. In Somalia, Al Shabaab can easily capitalize on the will of the people. The poor economic situation existing in Somalia gives the terrorist group the ability to easily recruit personnel who have a like minded Islamic ideology.

As we evaluate Al Shabaab's operating environment in Somalia we can then develop policy options that can address the issue which will be discussed further in chapter 4. The environment that terrorist groups operate provides them with the infrastructure to gain strength, increase capacity, and extend their reach more than any other single factor. ―Therefore, there are vulnerabilities that terrorist organizations have and the challenge to the United States is to put these vulnerabilities at risk. Threaten the terrorists groups where it hurts. Find what they care about and go after it."[25] Denying terrorist groups this safe haven can significantly reduce the terror threat to the United

---

[23] Szrom, 9.

[24] Horwitz, 138.

[25] Ibid, 139.

States. The ungoverned space provided by Somalia may be vulnerable to a wide variety of both military and intelligence options. A systematic approach that uses the full range of all military, diplomatic, informational, and economic measures to deny this environment would disrupt the terror threat we face.

CHAPTER 2: THREAT TO THE HOMELAND AND WESTERN INTERESTS

Security - Never permit the enemy to acquire an unexpected advantage

- Joint Pub 3.0

Threat

Today the threat is not across the ocean in some far distant region, but growing within our hometowns, communities, and schools. Three hundred people nearly died over the skies of Michigan on Christmas Day, 2009 when a terrorist attempted to blow up a plane destined for Detroit.[1] The terrorist, Umar Farouk Abdulmutallab, was an Al Qaeda (AQ) operative that had just departed terrorist training camps in the Arabian Peninsula. The camp where he trained resembles the camps that exist today in Somalia that are recruiting U.S. citizens in the Somali diasporas. Surprisingly, this attack took the country by surprise. The Somali diasporas which are found in many of our country's large cities and population centers are the targets for recruitment by Al Qaeda to plan and carry out terrorist attacks here at home within our own borders. This chapter will describe this threat in detail by discussing the current assessment as well as citing specific examples of individuals that have been recruited by Al Qaeda and describe in detail how and why this occurred in order to offer recommendations on intervention.

---

[1] Christopher Harnisch, *The Terror Threat from Somalia: The internationalization of Al Shabaab*, American Enterprise Institute, February 12, 2010.1.

The most valuable asset that Al Shabaab has at its disposal is foreign fighters, many of whom are from the United States. Before these U.S. citizens depart our borders to travel to Somalia in support of *Jihad* in the Al Shabaab terrorist training camps, they already possess a deadly weapon and that is a U.S. passport and legal residency. Armed with U.S. travel documents and incumbent knowledge of U.S. immigrations procedures afford them an unencumbered return.

The potential for future violent extremist acts is present. To date, the U.S. has disrupted attacks by individuals who were plotting attacks; however the threat is growing and gaining strides in both technical and tactical expertise. On July 11, 2010, the Somali terrorist group Al Shabaab carried out multiple suicide bombings in Kampala, Uganda. An estimated 76 people, including one American, were killed and more than 80 injured. The United Nations, the African Union, and the United States condemned the terrorist attacks and more than 20 suspects were arrested and imprisoned in Uganda.[2]

The FBI and U.S. Department of Homeland Security have warned that ―Al Shabaab's actions in Uganda could signal the group's capability of launching a successful attack beyond Africa, and even in the United States."[3] This attack should be considered a warning to the United States that it is only a matter of time before the terrorists groups in Somalia develop the capacity to move these attacks to our front door. Al Shabaab has made clear its desire and intention to strike beyond the borders of Somalia and this capability exists due to the safe haven in Somalia. Currently Al Shabaab has the means

---

[2] Ted Dagne, *Somalia: Current Conditions and Prospects for a Lasting Peace*, Specialist in African Affairs, Congressional Research Service, August 31, 2011, 2.

[3] Stephanie Hanson, Al-Shabaab, Council on Foreign Relations, August 10, 2011, http://www.cfr.org/somalia/al-shabaab/p18650 (accessed September 13, 2011).

to plan, prepare and execute such an attack.   It partners with and is loyal to AQ. It continuously strives to earn the respect and recognition of AQ's senior leadership. America cannot afford to ignore the threat posed by Al Shabaab.[4]

Again, Director Lieter from the National Counterterrorism Center (NCTC) commented, "The U.S. government has largely – not completely, but largely – focused its counterterrorism efforts on what the enemy looks like today." [5] This policy to date has proven effective; however the U.S. needs to think about what the enemy will look like tomorrow. As Al Qaeda changes, the U.S. government will also have to shift its focus to ensure that we are addressing the newly transformed Al Qaeda and its dispersed view of global *jihad* before they start to rise again.[6]

Somalia Diasporas

Diasporas provide a source of recruits, training, finance, arms, and logistics for the terrorist group. In 2009, Osama Bin Laden reached out to the Somalis stating, "You are one of the important armies in the Mujahid Islamic battalion," and encouraged the Somali diaspora "to rally around and help their brothers the honest Mujahideen."[7] In the case of Islamic terrorism, this form of sanctuary has been boosted by the emergence of a

---

[4] Harnisch, 2.

[5] Remarks by Honorable Michael E. Leiter, Director National Counter Terrorism Center at the Aspen Institute, April 9, 2009, http://www.dni.gov/speeches/20090409_speech.pdf (accessed August 23, 2011).

[6] Ibid.

[7] U.S. House of Representatives Committee on Homeland Security, Majority Investigative Report, *Al Shabaab: Recruitment and radicalization within the Muslim Community and the Threat to the Homeland*, Washington DC, July 27, 2011.

transnational *jihadi* network which creates synergy between local and global groups. [8] In a Majority Investigative Report on July 27, 2011, the Committee on Homeland Security listed a finding that stated there is a ‑looming danger of American Al Shabaab fighters returning to the U.S. to strike or help Al Qaeda and its affiliates attack the homeland."[9] The report discusses active Al Shabaab recruitment and radicalization on Muslim Americans in Somali communities and listed the key facts below:

- At least 40 or more Americans have joined Al Shabaab;
- So many Americans have joined that at least 15 of them have been killed fighting with Al Shabaab, as well as three Canadians;
- Three Americans who returned to the U.S. were prosecuted, and one awaits extradition from the Netherlands;
- At least 21 or more American Shabaab members overseas remain unaccounted for and pose a direct threat to the U.S. homeland.[10]

NCTC Director Michael Leiter told the Senate Homeland Security and Governmental Affairs Committee that ‑the potential for Somali trainees to return to the United States or elsewhere in the West to launch attacks remains of significant concern."[11] Al Shabaab's U.S. based recruiting network is expanding its reach through the use of cyberspace. An estimated 1.5 million Somalis worldwide are using internet chat rooms sponsored by the Somali diaspora to stay abreast of reports on the Al Shabaab offensive against the TFG and AMISOM. The majority report stated that Somali field commanders are encouraging U.S. citizens to return to their home to fight *jihad.* The

---

[8] Horwitz, 147.

[9] U.S. House of Representatives Committee on Homeland Security, Majority Investigative Report, *Al Shabaab: Recruitment and radicalization within the Muslim Community and the Threat to the Homeland,* Washington DC, July 27, 2011.

[10] Ibid.

[11] Remarks by Honorable Michael E. Leiter, Director National Counter Terrorism Center at the Aspen Institute, April 9, 2009, http://www.dni.gov/speeches/20090409_speech.pdf (accessed August 23, 2011).

FBI, Department of Homeland Security, and Department of Justice are pursuing Al Shabaab's U.S. based recruitment network of Somali-Americans —who prey on fellow Muslims and converts to convince them to fund Al Shabaab operations or to directly take up arms." [12] The U.S. Somali diasporas have become the primary target for recruiting Western fighters to Al Shabaab's cause for specialized missions such as suicide bombings and for propaganda and recruiting tapes. It was noted that American recruits are the foreign fighters most touted by Shabaab in its propaganda.[13] American Mosques across the country have been used to conceal recruiting and fund raising. At times when local clerics who intervened to disrupt these nefarious activities, they were threatened or even assaulted by pro-Shabaab radicals.

The ability of Al Shabaab to both recruit and indoctrinate U.S. citizens to execute an attack against the U.S. is clearly present. Christopher Harnisch, a research analyst and Gulf of Aden team lead for the Critical Threats Project whose research focuses on AQ and its associated movements, stated —Al Shabaab is composed of both Somali and international militants, including dozens from the United States. The group has threatened to attack the United States, and it has previously shown the ability to carry out its threats. The danger posed by Al Shabaab to America is real and imminent and there will be no excuse for being surprised when this group tries to attack the U.S."[14]

---

[12] U.S. House of Representatives Committee on Homeland Security, Majority Investigative Report, *Al Shabaab: Recruitment and radicalization within the Muslim Community and the Threat to the Homeland*, Washington DC, July 27, 2011, 3.

[13] Ibid, 4.

[14] Harnisch, 1.

Recruitment

As discussed earlier, Al Shabaab continues to work tirelessly from their safe haven in Somalia to become a terrorist network with international influence. It is estimated that the Somali community in the United States could be as high as 200,000 people. The recruitment efforts of Al Shabaab has successfully convinced dozens of Americans and Canadians to travel abroad to help fight in Somalia. So far, the group has not successfully attacked American targets, but their effort to recruit Americans shows that they have international aspirations.

Fueled by anti-Western narratives, home-grown radicalism and recruitment continues to increase in the United States. Steven Emerson, an internationally recognized expert on terrorism and national security, describes the phenomenon the United States is facing. Our country is deeply diverse religiously and ethnically and these groups still have ties to their home countries. Emerson states that —nomally this situation is not only harmless, but beneficial to the American fabric." He continues by stating that Osama Bin Laden's notorious February 1998 *fatwa* – an Islamic religious proclamation- declaring war on the United States has awakened a variety of radical extremists and recently individuals and groups have not only heard the call, but answered it.[15] —Foreign fighters have traveled to Somalia to fight with Al Shabaab, as have Somalis from the United Kingdom and the United States and we have seen an increasing number of individuals here in the United States become captivated by extremist ideologies or causes," said White House National

---

[15] Jeffery H. Horwitz, *Pirate, Terrorists and Warloard* (New York: Skyhorse Publishing, 2009), 205.

Security Adviser John Brennan in a May 2010 speech, noting, among others, five Somali-Americans that left Minnesota to fight in Somalia. [16]

U.S. Citizens

In 2008, Shirwa Ahmed, an American college student became the first U.S. citizen suicide bomber when he killed himself in Somalia. The suicide bomber was an American-Somali from Minneapolis who left the U.S. to take part in a suicide attack. This attack should raise fears in the U.S. If an American citizen can be radicalized to conduct an attack overseas, how long will it be before these attacks strike us within our borders. Since the first attack in 2008, two additional U.S. citizens of Somali descent have also carried out attacks: Farah Mohamed Belidi also from Minneapolis and another Al Shabaab fighter whose name has never been announced publically. Reportedly, over a dozen Somali youth from Minneapolis have left the United States, and some community leaders believe they went to Somalia to join the insurgency. There is no clear evidence of how many and for what purpose these Somalis left Minneapolis."[17]

A highly visible recruit is the U.S. born Abu Mansoor Al-Amriki, also known as Omar Shafik Hammami, who joined Al Shabaab in 2007."[18] Al-Amriki, from Daphne,

---

[16] Remarks by Assistant to the President for Homeland Security and Counterterrorism John Brennan at CSIS, *Securing the Homeland by Renewing American Strength, Resilience and Values,* May 26, 2010, http://www.whitehouse.gov/the-press-office/remarks-assistant-president-homeland-security-and-counterterrorism-john-brennan-csi (accessed September 13, 2011).

[17] Young Somali Men Missing from Minneapolis," *USA Today*, November 27, 2008. http://www.usatoday.com/news/nation/2008-11-26-missing-somalis_N.htm (accessed September 14, 2011).

[18] Stephanie Hanson, *Al-Shabaab*, Council on Foreign Relations, August 10, 2011, http://www.cfr.org/somalia/al-shabaab/p18650 (accessed September 13, 2011).

Alabama has been featured on numerous propaganda videos espousing *jihadist* idealism specifically justifying the September 11, 2001 terror attacks. Al-Amriki, an Alabama-raised Southern Baptist convert to Islam, has become one of Al Shabaab's recruiting success stories. He rose to become one of Al Shabaab's field commanders and has been seen on propaganda videos where he swore blood revenge against the United States for the May 1, 2011 killing of Osama Bin Laden by U.S. Special Operations Forces. Al-Amriki said, ―My Allah accept our dear beloved Sheikh and cause our swords to become instruments of his avenging," in a communiqué Al Shabaab released on May 11, 2011.[19] Counterterrorism officials believe that Al-Amriki poses a direct threat to the U.S. homeland with his ability to assist Al Shabaab, core Al Qaeda or AQAP with plots targeting the United States or its interests, but more importantly, Al-Amriki has become a source of inspiration for *jihadis*.

On February 2, 2009, Director of National Intelligence Dennis Blair at a Senate Select Committee on Intelligence hearing stated, ―We judge most Al Shabaab and East Africa based Al Qaeda members will remain focused on regional objectives in the near-term. Nevertheless, East Africa-based Al Qaeda leaders or Al Shabaab may elect to redirect to the homeland some of the Westerners, including North Americans, now training and fighting in Somalia."[20]

On August 5, 2010, more than a dozen Somali Americans and permanent residents were arrested. Attorney General Eric Holder announced that ―14 people are being

---

[19] U.S. House of Representatives Committee on Homeland Security, Majority Investigative Report, *Al Shabaab: Recruitment and radicalization within the Muslim Community and the Threat to the Homeland*, Washington DC, July 27, 2011.

[20] Director of National Intelligence Dennis C. Blair, Annual Threat Assessment of the U.S. Intelligence Community for the Senate Select Committee on Intelligence, February 2, 2010, 4.

charged with providing support to Al Shabaab. Two indictments unsealed in Minnesota states that Amina Farah Ali and Hawo Mohamed Hassan raised funds for Al Shabaab." The indictment states that 12 money transfers were made in 2008 and 2009. Holder stated at a press conference that —the indictments unsealed today shed further light on a deadly pipeline that has routed funding and fighters to the Al Shabaab terror organization from cities across the United States."[21]

Numerous counterterrorism officials raised concern over the increase in travel of U.S. citizens to Somalia. Somali-Americans from Minneapolis, Boston, Seattle, Washington, DC, San Diego and Columbus have traveled back to their homeland, many of which are on legitimate business or visiting relatives, but the challenge is to determine those who may be traveling to support Al Shabaab. Due to the lack of a functioning government and no immigration control, it is essentially impossible to determine the minority of Somali travelers from the U.S. who are going to support terror groups or join training camps.

Some observers and security officials estimate that there are several hundred foreign fighters in Somalia and U.S. officials have long expressed concern about the presence of known terrorist individuals in Somalia. Some observers contend that Somalia is being used as a transit and hiding place. In May 2009, a spokesman of Al Shabaab admitted that foreign fighters have joined the fighting. According to Sheik Husayn Fidow, —the Muslim people of Somalia have asked for assistance from other Muslim nations worldwide."[22]

---

[21] Ted Dagne, *Somalia: Current Conditions and Prospects for a Lasting Peace*, Specialist in African Affairs, Congressional Research Service, August 31, 2011, 5.

[22] Ibid.

In May 2008, Abdisalan Hussein Ali, who was born in Somalia but raised in Minneapolis, disappeared from Minnesota. On October 29, 2011 he resurfaced in devastating fashion. He was one of two suicide bombers among a force of militants disguised in Somali Army uniforms who attacked a military base of African Union peacekeepers in Mogadishu where ten people died. Abdisalan Hussein Ali is the fourth Somali-American to launch a suicide attack in Somalia.[23] Department of Homeland Security (DHS) Secretary Janet Napolitano said, "It's consistent with something we have been raising for months, which is a growth of Americans or U.S. persons who have become radicalized and this is a fundamental change in how we have seen terrorism [since] the attacks of 9/11."[24] Since 2006 as many as 30 young Somali men have left the United States to fight in Somalia which drives the need for a comprehensive review of U.S. policy on the Somali diasporas and the recruitment of U.S. citizens.

We must bring to bear resident capabilities to build resilience within our communities here at home against AQ inspired radicalization, recruitment, and mobilization to violence. Although increasing our engagement and partnership with communities can help protect them from the influence of Al Shabaab, we must ensure that we remain engaged in the full range of community concerns and interests. Just as the terrorist threat we face in the United States is multifaceted and cannot be reduced to a single group or community, so must our efforts to counter it not be reduced to a one-size-fits-all approach. We must support community leaders as they develop solutions tailored to their

---

[23] Al Shabaab: Suicide Bomber in Somalia Was American, ABC News http://abcnews.go.com/Blotter/al-shabab-suicide-bomber-somalia-american/story?id=14851524 (accessed October 31, 2011).

[24] Ibid.

own particular circumstances as a critical part of our whole-of-government approach that contributes to our counterterrorism goals.[25]

---

[25] U.S. President, *National Strategy for Counterterrorism*, Washington DC: Government Printing Office, June 2011, 9.

CHAPTER 3: SOMALIA TRAINING CAMPS

"Once one has decided to invade a country, one must not be afraid to deliver battle, and one should seek out the enemy everywhere to fight him" [1]

- **J.F.C. Fuller**

Establishment

Previous chapters discussed the current situation in Somalia as well as the recruitment and radicalization of U.S. citizens who have joined Al Shabaab in *Jihad*. This chapter will focus on how Al Shabaab is ―operationalizing" their terrorist network through established training camps in Somalia. Al Shabaab training camps emerged from training sessions attended in Afghanistan camps by senior leaders such as Mukhtar Rowbow and Aden Ayro. These key leaders then returned to Somalia and pioneered tactics which include suicide bombing and honing *Jihadist* ideology.[2] Key Al Shabaab leaders have publically aligned themselves with AQ and operate multiple training camps in Somalia with AQ's direct support and participation.[3] These camps, protected by the safe haven of Somalia, potentially house the terrorist that will launch the next attack on U.S. soil.

These senior leaders that are veterans of the Afghanistan and Pakistan training camps offer Al Shabaab valuable advantages. In these camps during the early stages of the U.S. led Operation Enduring Freedom, they gained the skills and tactics to fight guerilla style irregular warfare against a conventional enemy. Second, while in these camps, senior Al

---

[1] J.F.C. Fuller, *The Conduct of War*, (Da Capo Press, New Brunswick, New Jersey), 49.

[2] Jane's Terrorism and Insurgency Center, Shabaab Assimilates Rival, February 3, 2011. http://jtic.janes.com (accessed October 15, 2011).

[3] *2010 Posture Statement – United States Africa Command*, Statement of General William E. Ward, USA, Commander United States Africa Command to The House Armed Services Committee, 9-10 March 2010.

Shabaab leaders establish key contacts and learn to develop terrorist networks and contacts. Lastly, and possibly the most important, they learn how to operate successful training camps which we now see in Somalia. A September 2009 video released by Al Shabaab showed training camps in Somalia that frightfully resembled the camps in Afghanistan.[4]

The relationship between Al Qaeda and Al Shabaab manifested itself in the development of militant training camps similar to those that developed in Pakistan's tribal areas. These camps have raised red flags throughout the intelligence community. ―Al Shabaab benefits from the technical assistance of veterans of the wars in Iraq, Afghanistan, and Pakistan."[5] Equally concerning is that intelligence officials are now following about two dozen individuals from the U.S. that may be affiliated with Al Shabaab that have recently trained at these camps. These camps have attracted foreign fighters coming from the Somali diaspora in the United States, other African countries, and the Middle East.

Western intelligence agencies expressed concern over the presence of veteran foreign Jihadists in Somalia that give the terrorist group access to subject matter experts in explosives and small arms tactics who were able to train corps cadre in the skills to conduct asymmetric warfare. Media reports in November 2010 alleged that Al Shabaab recruited approximately 120 females and trained them on reconnaissance and intelligence gathering as well as techniques on obtaining and transporting explosives.[6] The Al Shabaab training camp in Lower Shabelle was designed to support hundreds of recruits

---

[4] Harnisch, 20.

[5] Ibid, 4.

[6] Jane's Terrorism and Insurgency Center, Shabaab Assimilates Rival, February 3, 2011. http://jtic.janes.com (accessed October 15, 2011).

and media reports claimed that the training would include small arms and explosives

courses with the intent to export the capabilities abroad.[7]

Al Shabaab operates training camps throughout much of the areas it controls. Al

Shabaab and Al Qaeda appear to be cooperating closely in their administration of the

training camps in southern Somalia. Some of these camps are reserved for imparting

basic ideological precepts and infantry skills to newly enlisted Somali militia members,

while others provide more advanced training in guerilla warfare, explosives, and

assassination."[8] The suicide attacks that targeted U.N. peacekeepers by Al Shabaab

militants who were tied to the training camps in Somalia reflect the growing capabilities

of the Al Shabaab terrorist organization. Hassan Dahir Aweys, a key terrorist leader in

Somalia who is on the U.S. government's list of terrorists, publically endorsed the suicide

attacks and called for the Muslim brothers to continue suicide attacks and the fight

against Muslim enemies. Intelligence officials report that Al Shabaab has the funds,

weapons, technical expertise, and human resources needed at these camps to conduct

operations. They raise money by taxing international aid organizations, collecting zakat

from citizens, receiving remittances from abroad, and receiving financial support from

Eritrea." Al Shabaab has displayed both large and small arms in its videos, and it has

proven its ability to succeed in battle against both conventional and irregular enemies.[9]

As mentioned previously, Al Shabaab claimed responsibility for the triple suicide blasts

---

[7] Ibid.

[8] Committee on Foreign Relations, *Al Qaeda in Yemen and Somalia: A ticking Time Bomb,* A Report to the Committee on Foreign Relations, 111th Congress, 2d Session, January 21, 2010. 15.

[9] Harnisch, 4.

that killed 76 people in Uganda's capital, Kampala. The Pakistan-style terror training camps planned, prepared and coordinated these attacks.

Al Qaeda Senior Leader Support

Numerous senior Al Shabaab leaders; the late Saleh Nabhan, Mukhtar Robow and Abu Mansur, have added credibility to these camps. Video clips that were released include short clips of Nabhan meeting with Shabaab spokesman, aka Abu Mansur, and training *Jihadist* at a terror training camp. He declares that the camps are open for anyone and calls for Muslim youth in Africa to come to Somalia. "Oh Muslim youth everywhere, don't forget the calls of your brothers in Somalia," he said. "What are you waiting for if you do not wage Jihad now? When will you wage Jihad? Oh Muslim youth!"[10] Prosecutors said the first group of Minnesotans under Mohamed Aided built a desert training camp and were taught terror tactics by top Shabaab leaders including Saleh Ali Saleh al-Nabhan, a Kenyan who also was a senior Al Qaeda operative with ties to violent Islamic extremists throughout the Horn of Africa region." (In late 2009, U.S. Special Operations Forces killed Nabhan in Somalia, according to press reports.)[11] As recently as December 2010, local Al Shabaab commander, Hassan Yaqub Ali reached out

---

[10] Grace, Nick, The Long War Journal, Shabaab reaches out to Al Qaeda senior leaders, announces death al Sudani, September 2, 2008, http://www.longwarjournal.org/archives/2008/09/shabab_reaches_out_t.php (accessed October 7, 2011).

[11] U.S. House of Representatives Committee on Homeland Security, Majority Investigative Report, *Al Shabaab: Recruitment and radicalization within the Muslim Community and the Threat to the Homeland*, Washington DC, July 27, 2011.

to citizens in Kismayu to enroll in the terrorist training camps. Ali stated, ―We like all types of people [such as] teachers, students and businessmen to be Shabaab fighters."[12]

Indoctrination

As Al Shabaab's power and influence expands in the region so too does the threat for attacks against Western interests. While the U.S. acknowledges that AQ activity in Somalia is present, the U.S. has for the most part overlooked the region. A U.S. State Department official indicated that Al Shabaab is showing signs of increased centralization through their own style of governance and indoctrination. Al Shabaab is trying to embed its Islamist ideology within the society by re-training Somali clerics through a seven month training camp called the Azzam training center.[13] The same process is happening on the military front with Al Shabaab using training camps to indoctrinate recruits. A senior U.S. terrorism expert described that the core of their training structure is to create a force that is ideologically committed to *Jihad*. These camps, bolstering its ideology by recruiting foreigners and Westerners, suggest the majority of the foreign fighters are ethnic Somalis drawn from diaspora communities. A regional analyst outlined their advantages, ―The expatriate Somalis are highly prized by Al Shabaab because when they return to Somalia they can quite easily be isolated and indoctrinated."[14] He continues by stating, ―They are increasingly able to take youths who

---

[12] Jane's Terrorism and Insurgency Center, Local Shabaab Commander calls for Citizens to Enroll in Training Camps, Decenmebr 9, 2010. http://jtic.janes.com (accessed October 15, 2011).

[13] Jane's Terrorism and Insurgency Center, Shabaab Assimilates Rival, February 3, 2011.

[14] Ibid.

have been dislocated from their families and indoctrinate them, teaching them a whole new narrative of Somali history, of Islamist Ideology." [15] A recent example of the success of this indoctrination was the Kampala bombings in 2010. Foreign fighters that were recruited, indoctrinated, and trained in the Somalia training camps organized and conducted these attacks.

The recruiting and indoctrination strategy remains vague; however three key themes are present. Al Shabaab surrogates attempt to indoctrinate Somali youth throughout the country in the diasporas by convincing them that it is their duty to fight and it is believed that some Somali religious leaders remain complicit in the indoctrination effort. The next technique that has proven successful is for prominent Somali role models to reach out and forge bonds to get Somali youths to join Al Shabaab. This last technique has been used to intimidate and threaten families of the recruits to allow them to join the fight. Those who speak out against Al Shabaab are labeled as traitors to the community.[16]

The president of the TFG, Sheikh Sharif, estimates that approximately 1,000 foreigners belong to Al Shabaab's ranks, many of which are ethnic Somalis from the diaspora. Al Shabaab's foreign fighters are valuable assets because they bring the desire to conduct suicide missions and they already have the required documents facilitating international travel to conduct an attack outside Somalia, especially on an American target. If successful, an attack on the U.S. homeland would earn the group further praise from Al Qaeda's leadership and legitimize it as contributor to the global jihad resulting in

---

[15] Jane's Terrorism and Insurgency Center, Shabbab Assimilates Rival, February 3, 2011. http://jtic.janes.com (accessed October 15, 2011).

[16] Christopher Harnisch, *The Terror Threat from Somalia: The Internationalization of Al Shabaab*, American Enterprise Institute, February 12, 2010, 31.

an influx of funds and foreign fighters. The concern to the United States is that Al

Shabaab has made it clear that it intends to strike beyond Somalia's borders.[17] Al

Shabaab poses a real and imminent threat to the United States and perhaps the most

alarming for our policy makers is that Al Shabaab has demonstrated its capacity to carry

out its threats.

---

[17] Ibid.

CHAPTER 4: U.S. POLICY

"The first, the supreme, the most far-reaching act of judgment that the statesman and the commander have to make is to establish…the kind of war in which they are embarking."[1]

- Clausewitz

Approach

Terrorist groups abroad have lent support to attempted attacks on the American homeland three times between 2010 and 2011 and the current administration under President Obama has not yet conducted a significant, systematic review of its approach to this threat. As noted by U.S. Assistant Secretary of State for African Affairs Johnnie Carson, the Obama administration's policy towards Somalia pursues a two-track policy in order to find a lasting solution to Somalia's crisis. He states, ―In the first track, the United States will continue to support the Transitional Federal Government (TFG), and in the second, it will engage current "governments" in Somaliland, Puntland, and other regional or clan entities."[2] This chapter will conduct a review of current U.S. policy on Somalia in order to determine specific shortfalls that address threats to the homeland emanating from Somalia. The analysis will focus on strategic guidance at the administration policy level which includes the National Security Strategy (NSS) and the

---

[1] Carl Von Clausewitz, *On War*, (Random House, New York, 1993), 100.

[2] Liban, Said, *U.S. Dual-Track Policy in Somalia*, November 24, 2010, http://www.worldpress.org/Africa/3657.cfm, (Accessed December 1, 2011).

National Strategy for Combating Terrorism, as well as strategic guidance from the Secretary of Defense and the Chairman of the Joint Chiefs of Staff (CJCS) which will include the National Defense Strategy, National Military Strategy, and the National Military Strategic Plan for the War on Terrorism.

Charlie Szrom from the American Enterprise Institute states, "Defeating the militant Islamist network led by Al Qaeda requires a nuanced strategy that supports the appropriate combination and prioritization of policies and approaches for each environment in which an Al Qaeda affiliate or franchise operates."[3] Currently our government has failed to implement a detailed or comprehensive strategy focused on the threats emanating from Somalia and this failure requires urgent attention because terrorist groups based abroad have been linked to three attacks against the American homeland in the past year.

Time may be the best ally of the terrorists and too often the United States is quick to lose sight on its objectives. Following the World Trade Center attacks, President George W. Bush in a speech to the U.S. Congress stated the United States' position on terrorists and those countries that harbor them:

> We will starve terrorists of funding, turn them one against another, drive them from place to place, until there is no refuge or rest. And we will pursue nations that provide aid or safe haven to terrorism. Every nation, in every region, now has a decision to make. Either you are with us, or you are with the terrorists. From this day forward, any nation that continues to harbor or support terrorism will be regarded by the United States as a hostile regime.[4]

---

[3] Charlie Szrom, *Al Queda's Operating Environment – A New Approach to the War on Terror*, American Enterprise Institute, March 2011.1.

[4] President George W. Bush, Speech to Congress, September 20, 2001, http://www.pearlharbor.org/speech-bush-sep-20-2001.asp (accessed October 16, 2011).

As we look at Somalia today, do these statements still hold true? Clearly Somalia has provided refuge for terrorists; more so, the failed state has provided ideal conditions for terrorists to not only seek refuge, but to develop networks and training camps extending their reach potentially to our borders. Throughout the analysis of current U.S. strategy, three key tasks resonate and underpin our strategy against Al Qaeda and they include disrupt, dismantle and defeat terrorists in order to ensure the safety of U.S. citizens and our other national interests.

United States and Somalia

The Obama administration actively supports the Transitional Federal Government (TFG) in an effort to try and contain the terrorist threat that is present. The U.S. has passed several resolutions and conducted numerous Congressional hearings on the issue; however no clear policy has surfaced. In August 2009, Secretary of State Hillary Clinton met with the TFG President, Sheik Shaif Ahmad and expressed U.S. support for the TFG. Later in September 2009, President Ahmad traveled to the United States to address the U.N. General Assembly and went to Washington for a meeting with U.S. officials in an effort to bolster support for both the TFG and the challenges surmounting with Al Shabaab and yet, little support has been delivered from countries other than the United States and the participants in AMISOM. The United States has provided an estimated $151.1 million in 2010 and $82.3 million in 2011 and the Obama Administration requested $91.8 Million from the U.N. for AMISOM in 2012.[5]

---

[5] Ted Dagne, *Somalia: Current Conditions and Prospects for a Lasting Peace*, Specialist in African Affairs, Congressional Research Service, August 31, 2011.3.

Policy Rhetoric

The recent plots against the United States have forced White House leadership and policy makers to reconsider U.S. policy on Somalia. Unfortunately key policy makers have only applied rhetoric to the problem with no substantial improvement on U.S. policy. This was highlighted in March 2011 by comments from the White House National Security Adviser John Brennan in a speech delivered at the Center for Research and Strategic Studies (CRSS) where he stated ―to deny Al Qaeda and its affiliates safe haven, we will take the fight to Al Qaeda and its extremist affiliates wherever they plot and train… we are helping governments build their capacity to provide for their own security, to help them root out the Al Qaeda cancer that has manifested itself within their borders and to help them prevent it from returning."[6] He continues, ―We have a clear mission. We will not simply degrade Al Qaeda's capabilities or simply prevent terrorist attacks against our country or citizens. We will not merely respond after the fact—after an attack has been attempted. Instead, the United States will disrupt, dismantle, and ensure a lasting defeat of Al Qaeda and violent extremist affiliates." [7] These are strong words; however there have been no significant changes in U.S. policy on Somalia, yet the threat continues to grow there.

---

[6] Remarks by Assistant to the President for Homeland Security and Counterterrorism John Brennan at CRSS, *Securing the Homeland by Renewing American Strength, Resilience and Values*, May 26, 2010, http://www.whitehouse.gov/the-press-office/remarks-assistant-president-homeland-security-and-counterterrorism-john-brennan-csi (accessed September 13, 2011).

[7] Ibid.

Additionally, comments made by Honorable Michael E. Leiter, Director of the National Counterterrorism Center (NCTC) at the Aspen Institute on April 9, 2009 also highlighted points of concern. The purpose of the NCTC is to ―Lead our nation's effort to combat terrorism at home and abroad by analyzing the threat, sharing that information with our partners, and integrating all instruments of national power to ensure unity of effort.‖[8] In his address, Director Leiter states, ―I think it's important to remind people what we do because frankly, even the people with whom I work on a daily basis aren't always sure.‖ He goes on to say, ―So what I have said often and I'll continue to say it is I think an attack from homegrown terrorists may be the most likely terrorist event that the U.S. experiences in the future.‖ He continues, ―we have seen a very, very small percentage of individuals of Somali descent who have come to identify with extremists in Somalia, be they Al Shabaab or potentially elements of Al Qaeda.‖[9]

Following the Al Shabaab attacks in Uganda that were discussed in chapter 3, the House of Representatives passed Security Resolution 1538 stating that the United States, ―strongly condemns Al Shabaab's destabilizing role in Somalia and the region; recognizes the importance of Uganda's peacekeeping efforts in Somalia and calls on the Administration to work with the international community to address the security threat emanating from Somalia.‖[10] These attacks were conducted in July 2010 and should have been a warning to the U.S. on the potential that exists for Al Shabaab to expand its reach

---

[8] The National Center Terrorism Center Mission Statements, http://www.nctc.gov/ (Accessed September 20, 2011).

[9] Remarks by Honorable Michael E. Leiter, Director National Counter Terrorism Center at the Aspen Institute, April 9, 2009, http://www.dni.gov/speeches/20090409_speech.pdf (accessed August 23, 2011).

[10] U.S. House of Representatives Resolution 1538, Condemning the July 11, 2010, terrorist attacks in Kampala, Uganda. 111th Congress, 2d Session, July 20, 2010.

to our borders, yet outside the Washington Capitol region dialogue, no substantive action has occurred.

National Security Strategy

As described in the introduction narrative of the March 2010 National Security Strategy (NSS), the United States faces a broad and complex array of challenges. American interests are enduring and first and foremost are the security of the United States, its citizens, and U.S. allies and partners.[11] In the NSS, it states that the Administration has no greater responsibility than the safety and the security of the American people and that the U.S. will disrupt, dismantle, and defeat Al Qaeda and its affiliates though a comprehensive strategy that denies them safe haven, strengthens our front line partners, and secures our homeland. Al Shabaab continues to gain both strength and momentum due to a lack of implementing specific U.S. policy. The most significant action taken by the U.S. was on 29 February 2008 when the U.S. government designated Al Shabaab as a Foreign Terrorist Organization. However, since that time little action has been taken against Al Shabaab and the potential threat emanating from Somalia.

Chapter III of the NSS, Advancing Our Interests, devotes an entire section to disrupting, dismantling and defeating Al Qaeda and its violent extremist affiliates as well as clearly identifying measures, that if implemented would be successful in Somalia.

---

[11] U.S. President, *National Security Strategy*, Washington DC: Government Printing Office, May 2010, 7.

There are three key points in the NSS that address methods to affect a successful strategy for disrupting and containing the terrorist threat in Somalia.

First, we must leverage the full spectrum of intelligence, law enforcement and homeland capabilities. Specific actions include better coordination with partner nations to identify and track not only specific terrorist individuals, but focus on the financial network as well to prevent terrorist travel.

Second, we must deny Al Qaeda the ability to threaten American people, our allies, our partners and our interests overseas.[12] Al Qaeda and its affiliates such as Al Shabaab must not be permitted to gain or maintain the capacity to plan and launch international attacks, especially against the U.S. homeland. The NSS states, —We must deny these groups the ability to conduct operational plotting from any locale, or to recruit, train, and position operatives, including those from North America and Europe."[13] As discussed earlier, Al Shabaab has been successful in each of these areas. As recently as October 24, 2011, Al Shabaab claimed responsibility for attacks in Kenya. Kenyan authorities have increased security in the capital, following a grenade attack at a bar in downtown Nairobi that wounded 13 people. The attack came after Somali militant group Al Shabaab warned it would retaliate for an ongoing Kenyan military incursion into Somalia.[14]

Third, we must deny terrorists safe havens and strengthen at risk states. Wherever Al Qaeda or its affiliates establish a safe haven and the NSS specifically lists Somalia, the

---

[12] U.S. President, *National Security Strategy*, Washington DC: Government Printing Office, May 2010, 7.

[13] Ibid, 20.

[14] Grenade Attack in Kenya Follows Threats From al-Shabab, Voice in America, October 24, 2011. http://www.voanews.com/english/news/africa/Grenade-Attack-Wounds-13-in-Kenya-132429548.html (accessed October 24, 2011).

NSS states the U.S. will meet them with growing pressure. It is important to analyze in detail following aspects of the NSS:

> We also will strengthen our own network of partners to disable Al Qaeda's financial, human, and planning networks; disrupt terrorist operations before they mature; and address potential safe-havens before Al Qaeda and its terrorist affiliates can take root. These efforts will focus on information-sharing, law enforcement cooperation, and establishing new practices to counter evolving adversaries. We will also help states avoid becoming terrorist safe havens by helping them build their capacity for responsible governance and security through development and security sector assistance.[15]

The United States simply has failed to disrupt Al Shabaab's safe haven that allows them the ability to plan, train, recruit and execute terrorist attacks. Contrary to our NSS, Al Shabaab has matured and little to no change is evident from the financial aid directed towards Somalia. Millions of dollars have funneled into Somalia in support of partner nation efforts with no measurable success.

As recently as September 15, 2011 Charlie Savage of the *New York Times* reported on the Obama Administration's split over how much latitude the United States has to kill terrorists in Somalia. The discussion reveals the lack of political clarity on the issue between targeting specific individuals that has already occurred over 12 times and expanding the policy to focus on the ―rank and file‖ terrorists groups such as Al Shabaab. The dispute between the State Department and Pentagon is specifying the limits on the use of lethal force in the region and whether the administration can escalate the attacks beyond individuals to Somalia based Al Shabaab.[16] Senator Lindsey Graham, a South Carolina Republican on the Armed Services Committee stated, ―This is a worldwide

---

[15] U.S. President, *National Security Strategy*, Washington DC: Government Printing Office, May 2010, 21.

[16] The New York Times, White House Weighs Limits of Terror Fight, Charlie Savage, September 15, 2011. http://www.nytimes.com/2011/09/16/us/white-house-weighs-limits-of-terror-fight.html?pagewanted=all (accessed October 18, 2011).

conflict without borders," and that Congress may consider this issue as part of a pending

defense bill to use military force against low-level militants in places like Somalia. [17] It

is clearly articulated in the NSS that we will help states avoid becoming terrorist safe

havens by helping them build their capacity for responsible governance and security

through development and security sector assistance. No programs to date have

completed this task and Somalia continues to be a failed state providing a safe haven for

Al Shabaab.

The next section will further analyze the link of our May 2010 National Security

Strategy to that of the June 2011 National Strategy for Counterterrorism in an effort to

identify gaps and shortfalls in our approach on Somalia and Al Shabaab.

National Strategy for Counterterrorism

The National Strategy for Counterterrorism (NSCT) articulates the United States'

broad, sustained and integrated campaign against Al Qaeda, its affiliates and its

adherents, consistent with the President's enduring commitment to protect the American

people as outlined in his National Security Strategy. It formalizes the approach that

President Obama and his Administration have been pursuing and adapting to prevent

terrorist attacks and to defeat Al Qaeda. President Obama clearly specifies the task at

hand:

> Our terrorist adversaries have shown themselves to be agile and adaptive;
> defeating them requires that we develop and pursue a strategy that is even more
> agile and adaptive. To defeat Al Qaeda, we must define with precision and clarity

---

[17] Ibid.

who we are fighting, setting concrete and realistic goals tailored to the specific challenges we face in different regions of the world.[18]

As identified in the National Security Strategy, the NSCT addresses the threat we face and reiterates that our key tasks in achieving success are to disrupt, dismantle and defeat AQ and its affiliates. The NSCT lists four overarching principles that will guide U.S. counterterrorism efforts: adhering to U.S. core values, building security partnerships, applying CT tools and capabilities appropriately, and building a culture of resilience.[19] Of these four principles, two principles can be directly tied to Somalia which if implemented could prove successful in disrupting Al Shabaab in Somalia and these two are building security partnerships and applying CT tools and capabilities appropriately.

The United States alone cannot defeat Al Qaeda and Al Shabaab in Somalia, it will take partner nation cooperation with countries in the region that have a vested interest in the security and stability of the region. The African Union Mission in Somalia (AMISOM) contributing countries as well as those countries that border Somalia are but a few that offer partnership opportunities. Currently the United States has this capacity resident in Djibouti. The Combined Joint Task Force – Horn of Africa (CJTF-HOA) established in May 2003 at Camp Lemonnier, Djibouti was created for just this type of mission. CJTF-HOA's primary mission is to build partner nation capacity in order to promote regional security. This is completed in two ways. First by implementing professional military to military training focused on regional security and second, by partnering civil military operations that focus on meeting basic human needs and building

_____

[18] U.S. President, *National Strategy for Counterterrorism*, Washington DC: Government Printing Office, June 2011.

[19] Ibid, 4.

trust and confidence between the military and vulnerable populations.[20] CJTF-HOA will be further examined in chapter 5 in conjunction with the United States Africa Command's mission and priorities.

The next principle is applying CT tools and capabilities appropriately. As the Al Shabaab network continues to evolve in Somalia, the U.S. must continually evaluate the tools and capabilities that we can leverage in this fight. In order to disrupt and defeat the threat, we must pursue a ―Whole of Government" effort that integrates the capabilities and authorities of each of our departments and agencies.[21] A key statement in the NSCT addresses the weighing the costs and risks of its actions to those of inaction.[22] The recent attack in Kenya targeting Western interests is a prime example of the results of policy inaction. As Al Shabaab continues to develop capacity, these threats may soon reach our borders.

The NSCT lists key overarching goals that are nested in the principles that guide our counterterrorism efforts that we must achieve in order to successfully defeat Al Qaeda. These specific goals listed that can be linked to success in Somalia include:

- Protecting the American people
- Disrupt, degrade, dismantle, and defeat al-Qaeda and its affiliates and adherents
- Eliminate safe havens
- Build enduring counterterrorism partnerships and capabilities
- Degrade links between al-Qaeda and its affiliates and Adherents and

---

[20] Brian L. Losey, *Conflict Prevention in East Africa – the Indirect Approach*, Prism, Center for Complex Operations, Vol. 2, No. 2, March 2011, 80.

[21] U.S. President, *National Strategy for Counterterrorism*, Washington DC: Government Printing Office, June 2011, 7.

[22] Ibid.

- Deprive terrorists of their enabling means[23]

Successfully implementing these goals against Al Shabaab in Somalia can prevent the recurrence of an attack on the homeland by this group or one its affiliates. These goals would disrupt plots as well as constrain Al Shabaab's ability to plan for attacks by decreasing its security and freedom of maneuver in the Somalia safe haven. At the same time, the U.S. must be prepared to adjust its strategy to confront the evolving threat prompted in part by specific instances of successful attacks. However; the strategy must expand its focus to articulate the specific approaches we must take to counter AQ affiliates and adherents on the periphery of the major areas of Iraq and Afghanistan to the established affiliated groups in Somalia or individual adherents in the Homeland who may be mobilized to violence in AQ's name.[24] The principal focus of this counterterrorism strategy is the network that poses the most direct and significant threat to the United States—AQ, its affiliates and its adherents.

National Strategy for Homeland Security

Homeland security is a concerted national effort to prevent terrorist attacks within the United States, reduce America's vulnerability to terrorism, and minimize the damage to recover from attacks that do occur.[25] The importance of this strategy is stated in the first sentence, ―America is at war with terrorist enemies who are intent on attacking our

---

[23] Ibid, 9.

[24] Ibid, 19.

[25] U.S. President, *National Strategy for Homeland Security*, Homeland Security Council, Washington DC: Government Printing Office, October 2007, 3.

Homeland and destroying our way of life."[26] As we assess the threat to our homeland

emanating from Somalia, there are several key areas addressed in our National Strategy

for Homeland Security (NSHS) that are relevant. These include the overarching purpose

of the strategy, the impact of radicalization of the Somali diasporas within our cities,

terrorist travel, and degrading terrorist financial funding. Each of these areas, if

addressed in a comprehensive U.S. policy focused on Somalia and Al Shabaab would

prove critical to preventing an Al Shabaab or its affiliates from affecting an attack within

our borders.

The National Strategy for Homeland Security is a companion to the National

Strategy for Combating Terrorism addressed previously and the sections in both of these

strategy documents on preventing and disrupting terrorist attacks are complementary and

mutually reinforcing.[27] We are not immune to the emergence and radicalization of

homegrown terrorists who are influenced by Al Shabaab who spreads violent Islamic

extremism that is —driven by an undiminished strategic intent to attack our Homeland."[28]

The arrests and prosecution of several U.S. citizens who have become Islamic extremist

leads us to believe that others are present and have the same desire and radicalized

motivation to use violence in our country as legitimate means to achieve their goals. To

succeed on this front against Al Shabaab, we must eliminate perceptions and feelings of

social discrimination that generate a sense of alienation from our way of life that lures

vulnerable Somali youth to the Al Shabaab cause. Add to this, we must remove the

---

[26] Ibid, 1.

[27] Ibid, 15.

[28] U.S. President, *National Strategy for Homeland Security*, Homeland Security Council, Washington DC: Government Printing Office, October 2007, 9.

perceptions in political and economic inequality and dissatisfaction with foreign and domestic policy viewed as hostile to Muslims. A government policy that articulates this narrative through the Somali community leaders and family members will disrupt Al Shabaab radicalization and recruitment in our cities.

Denying terrorists the ability to travel internationally, specifically across and within our borders, will decrease their effectiveness and the NSHS addresses this issue through several initiatives for screening travelers. The issue with these programs, specifically the REAL ID Act [29] and US-VISIT program,[30] is that it will only affect non-U.S. citizens. As we have seen, countless U.S. citizens, who would be immune to these programs, have already successfully traveled to Somalia to train in Al Shabaab terrorist training camps and will not be challenged by these measures upon arrival.

For the NSHS to be successful, Congress must fulfill its responsibilities in a national effort to secure our Homeland and protect its citizens. Currently, Congress has failed to establish clear and consistent priorities or provide optimal oversight to secure our borders from an Al Shabaab attack.

Defense Strategy

Defense strategies must be nested in our National Security Framework. As we look for solutions to protect our Homeland from the threat that exists from Al Shabaab, it

---

[29] The REAL ID Act establishes Federal standards for State issued drivers licence and non driver's identification cards.

[30] The United States Visitor and Imigrant Status Indicator Technology (US-VISIT) program when fully implemented will create an entry and exit system that matches foreign traveler's arrival and departure records using biometrics to screen applicants for admission to the U.S.

is imperative that our military strategy incorporate the intent and guidance detailed from the Administration level documents. The Secretary of Defense provides guidance and direction for the military in the Quadrennial Defense Review (QDR). The QDR analyzes strategic objectives and potential military threats to our nation. In the 2010 QDR, unlike our national level strategies, surprisingly there is sparse attention directed at the potential threats that exist from the expansion of Al Qaeda from Iraq and Afghanistan into safe haven locations such as Somalia.

The 2010 QDR only addresses terrorist and safe havens in very broad terms, ―Terrorist groups seek to evade security forces by exploiting ungoverned areas as safe havens from which to recruit, indoctrinate, and train fighters, as well as to plan attacks on the U.S. and allied interests.‖[31] In a broad sweep, the QDR's primary capability to deter terrorist safe havens is through the use of security cooperation activities, ―the most dynamic in the coming years will be security force assistance (SFA) missions in a ―hands on‖ effort conducted primarily in host countries, to train, equip, advise, and assist those countries' forces in becoming more proficient at providing security to their populations and protecting their resources and territories.‖[32] As we look at Somalia and the status of AMISOM and the TFG, there has been little success at strengthening their capacity for internal security in the fight with Al Shabaab. Al Shabaab continues to capitalize on the safe haven in Somalia and attacks such as those in Uganda, Kenya and Mogadishu may only be the precursor of events to unfold in the U.S. unless our efforts are not increased to support the TFG and AMISOM with military capacity.

---

[31] Robert M. Gates, Quadrennial Defense Review Report, Washington DC: Government Printing Office, February 2010, 27.

[32] Ibid, 26.

The Chairman of the Joint Chiefs of Staff, Admiral Mullen, in the 2011 National Military Strategy of the United States clearly identifies the threat emanating specifically from Somalia and articulates options available to defeat violent extremism that if implemented would prove effective against Al Shabaab. On February 8, 2011, Admiral Mullen Stated, "Today, I released the 2011 National Military Strategy which provides a vision for how our Joint Force will provide the military capability to protect the American People, defend our Nation and allies, and contribute to our broader peace, security and prosperity while we continue to refine how we counter violent extremism."[33]

It is also important to note that this was the first update in over seven years (last released in 2004). The strategy clearly articulates the risk to the United States of failed states that offer safe havens for terror networks. Nested in the National Security Strategy and the QDR, the military strategy is in line with the national military objective to disrupt, dismantle, and defeat Al Qaeda and counter violent extremism. Admiral Mullen emphasizes that all measures taken must be in conjunction with our Allies and partner nations. He continues in stating, "Terrorists' abilities to remotely plan and coordinate attacks is growing and extending their operational reach while rendering targeting of their sanctuaries more difficult. Undeterred by the complexity of terrorist networks and in concert with our Allies and partners, we will be prepared to find, capture, or kill violent extremists wherever they reside when they threaten interests and citizens of America and our allies."[34] The strategy focuses on a whole-of-nation approach and establishing

___

[33] Council on Foreign Affairs, National Military Strategy of the United States of America, 2011, http://www.cfr.org/defense-strategy/national-military-strategy-united-states-america-2011/p24045 (accessed October 31, 2011).

[34] Chairman of the Joint Chiefs of Staff, *The National Strategy of the United States of America,* Washington, DC: Government Printing Office, February 2011, 6.

regional partnerships to erode terrorist support and source of legitimacy while at the same time improving relationships with the interagency. Lastly, the strategy states when directed, ‒we will provide capabilities to hold accountable any government or entity complicit in attacks against the United States."[35]

Policy Options

As noted, at the Administration level, no clear U.S. policy exists and for the past two years the United States has provided over $250 million in aid with no clear progress on containing the terrorist threat that exists in Somalia. Many observers believe that the solution lies in senior clan elder engagement as a means to resolve the political and security problems and that Al Shabaab can only be contained by another Islamist movement supported by clan elders. According to some experts, a targeted measure that includes sanctions and assassination of the most extreme elements of Al Shabaab could give rise for more moderate leaders to emerge.[36] The United States should seek a Somali led solution, both political and military. Only through a coalition of the TFG, Islamic courts, and other moderate Somali forces can the Al Shabaab terrorist network be contained. However, a review of our defense strategy offers numerous options that if implemented would prove successful in disrupting and dismantling Al Shabaab's terrorist network in Somalia. To build on the defense strategy, the next chapter will analyze the United States Africa Command (AFRICOM) strategy for the region.

---

[35] Ibid.

[36] Ted Dagne, *Somalia: Current Conditions and Prospects for a Lasting Peace*, Specialist in African Affairs, Congressional Research Service, August 31, 2011.16.

CHAPTER 5: AFRICOM – STRATEGY AND PRIORITIZATION

Posture

In recent years the United States has noted the increased strategic importance of Africa. Today, with the increasing threat of attacks within our borders, Africa wields mounting concern over violent extremist activities posed in the Somalia safe haven. The previous chapters discussed many key aspects of the crisis in Somalia; this chapter will focus on the United States Africa Command (AFRICOM) and its plan to disrupt, dismantle, and defeat the Al Qaeda and Al Shabaab terrorist networks that reside within its geographic area of operations. On February 6, 2007, the Bush Administration announced the creation of a new unified combatant command, U.S. Africa Command or AFRICOM, to promote U.S. national security objectives in Africa.[1] The mission of AFRICOM is to work in concert with other U.S. government agencies and international partners to conduct sustained security engagement through military-to-military programs, military-sponsored activities, and other military operations as directed to promote a stable and secure African environment in support of U.S. foreign policy.[2] This chapter will analyze the strategic plan for AFRICOM in order to determine if its objectives are nested in national and defense level strategy guidance. The Obama Administration's strategy for countering terrorism in Africa, as outlined in the 2011 National Strategy for

---

[1] Lauren Ploch, *Africa Command: U.S. Strategic Interests and the Role of the U.S. Military in Africa*, Congressional Research Service - RL34003, July 22, 2011, 1.

[2] United States Government Accounting Office, *Improved Planning, Training, and Interagency Collaboration Could Strengthen DOD's Efforts in Africa*, Defense Management, Report to the Subcommittee on National Security and Foreign Affairs on Oversight and Government Reform, House of Representative, GAO-10-794, July 2010, 3.

Counterterrorism, focuses on dismantling Al Qaeda elements in the region and empowering countries and local administrations to serve as countervailing forces to the supporters of Al Qaeda and the purveyors of instability that enable the transnational terrorist threat to persist."[3]

Atmospherics

On October 13, 2011 Secretary of Defense Leon Panetta warned of retreat from Africa. He fears that the looming defense budget cuts on the horizon will force a reduction in U.S. presence in many terrorist hotspots around the world, namely Africa. He continued by stating, "If you are talking about risk, part of the risk would be having less of a presence" in this area.[4] Both he and Army General Martin Dempsey, Chairman of the Joint Chiefs of Staff, testified that the Pentagon is conducting a strategic review to determine how to do more missions with fewer resources. The ability to target terrorist threats in Africa is critical to homeland security and General Dempsey emphasized the importance of the region specifically discussing Somalia and the AQ militants, "Our presence on the African continent is part of our network of building partners, of gaining intelligence and then when targeting approaches or targeting reaches the level of refinement, we can act on it."[5] The Commander of AFRICOM, General Carter Ham expressed mounting concern over the terrorist organization Al Shabaab who has publicly

---

[3] U.S. President, *National Strategy for Counterterrorism*, Washington DC: Government Printing Office, June 2011, 14.

[4] Leon Panetta , U.S. Secretary of Defense, *Panetta Warms of Retreat in Africa*, Washington Times, October 14, 2011, 1.

[5] Ibid.

and explicitly voiced intent to target the United States. In a *New York Times* interview on September 14, 2011 following the Al Shabaab attacks in Uganda, General Ham stated he was concerned about Al Shabaab's capability to extend these attacks beyond the regional areas in Africa to the United States. Pending the withdrawal of forces from Iraq and the reduction in American forces in Afghanistan, General Ham was optimistic that this may provide additional numbers of Special Operations Forces (SOF) to support AFRICOM's partner nation training mission lead by the Combined Joint Task Force – Horn of Africa (CJTF-HOA, this Task Force will be discussed in a separate section further in this chapter).[6]

AFRICOM Posture Statements – 2010 and 2011

In 2010 and 2011 the AFRICOM Commander, General William E. "Kip" Ward and General Carter F. Ham respectively, testified before the Congressional Armed Service Committee and presented the Africa Command Posture Statement. It has been a long-standing tradition that regional military commanders deliver a "posture statement" on their region of the world in public hearings to the U.S. Congress where they outline their priorities, objectives and strategy for their region. A review of the two most recent posture statements in 2010 and 2011 provide insights to the threat emanating from Somalia and the threat that Al Shabaab poses to the United States and its interests as well as programs that have been implemented to counter these threats.

---

[6] The New York Times, Three Terrorists Groups in Africa pose Threat to the U.S., American Commander says. September 14, 2011. http://www.nytimes.com/2011/09/15/world/africa/three-terrorist-groups-in-africa-pose-threat-to-us-general-ham-says html (accessed November 2, 2011).

In the 2010 Posture Statement, General Ward addresses violent extremism and transnational threats to the United States and specifically discusses concerns over the momentum that Al Shabaab gained when they aligned themselves with AQ and further expanded their capacity with the creation of multiple terrorists training camps in southern Somalia. There are two key successes in AFRICOM's approach that support the National Security Strategy and the Defense Strategy objective of sustained security in Somalia.

The first is the military-to-military engagement (mil-to-mil) and the second is capacity building programs. Each works effectively through coordination with interagency partners and regional cooperation. Emphasizing that the more the countries of East Africa work together, the greater the likelihood that Al Shabaab can be defeated and that Somalia can be stabilized.[7] The military-to-military (mil-to-mil) bilateral training events strengthen key relationships and familiarize partner nations such as Uganda and Burundi who are active supporters of the AMISOM peacekeeping mission with U.S. military techniques, tactics, and procedures that they can employ to address a broad range of security challenges which include countering Al Shabaab. In 2010, AFRICOM's mil-to-mil programs were the cornerstone for their engagement activities with over $6.3 million allocated.

AFRICOM's capacity building programs support the State Department and U.S. Embassy lead initiatives that include the following elements: information operations; train, advise, and assist activities; intelligence capacity building; coalition development

---

[7] 2010 Posture Statement – United States Africa Command, Statement of General William E. Ward, USA, Commander United States Africa Command to The House Armed Services Committee, 9-10 March 2010, 11.

and establishment of a regional computer based information network.[8] AMISOM, the multilateral African Union Mission in Somalia, is severely under-resourced, but essential in supporting the TFG in Somalia's security and stability. As AFRICOM prioritizes their efforts in the region, AMISOM and the TFG are critical. Currently AFRICOM provides military mentors to AMISOM, deploying forces focused on peacekeeping operations; however, this is only a starting point if the U.S. truly wants to defeat the Al Shabaab terrorist network in Somalia. The success of the TFG and AMISOM is directly related to disrupting both Al Shabaab and AQ terrorist networks in the Somalia safe haven and currently, the United States and AFRICOM's support is minimal having little to no direct impact on Al Shabaab terrorist operations.

The following year General Ham, who succeeded General Ward at the helm of AFRICOM, continued to press the fight for AFRICOM to defeat the terrorist threat emanating from Al Shabaab in Somalia in his 2011 Posture Statement to Congress. He highlighted in broad language the fact that Somalia is a failed state and that Al Shabaab's merger with AQ poses a direct threat to the U.S. and its interests; however, his address to Congress failed to provide any specific plan to disrupt the terror threat emanating from the Somalia safe haven as addressed the previous year by General Ward. General Ham states that U.S. Africa Command established the following theater objective ―Ensure that the AQ networks and associated violent extremist do not attack the United States."[9] Until recently, aside from a cursory discussion of multinational and interagency cooperation initiatives tied to countering the terrorist threat in East Africa, there was no

<hr>

[8] Ibid, 25.

[9] *2011 Posture Statement – United States Africa Command*, Statement of General Carter Ham, USA, Commander United States Africa Command to The House Armed Services Committee, April 5, 2011, 10.

concrete plan to meet the National Security and National Defense Strategy objectives to defeat, disrupt, and dismantle AQ and its Al Shabaab affiliate. However, as of November 2011, AFRICOM senior planners stated that they are readdressing the priorities on the continent and are dividing the continent into five separate regions and East Africa is the priority region among the five. In their operational approach two methods that are being implemented include strengthening partner nation defense capabilities and building partner security cooperation, both of which are nested in the National Military Strategy and the National Security Strategy. [10]

Combined Joint Task Force – Horn of Africa (CJTF-HOA)

Prior to the formation of Africa Command (AFRICOM), Department of Defense African regional coordination and efforts were directed by the U.S. Central Command (CENTCOM). Following the attacks of 9-11, CENTCOM established the Combined Joint Task Force – Horn of Africa (CJTF-HOA). CJTF-HOA's mission was to counter terrorists linked to AQ and in May 2003, the task force established its headquarters at Camp Lemonnier, Djibouti. CJTF-HOA is essential to AFRICOM's efforts to build the partner capacity necessary to counter violent extremism and address the East Africa regional security issues. CJTF-HOA has become the model for multinational and interagency collaboration which is the cornerstone to success in Somalia to defeat Al Shabaab. Recently they have played a key role in two important State Department

---

[10] This information was obtained from a video teleconference on November 21, 2011 between the Joint Forces Staff College at Norfolk, Virginia and the J5 planning leads from AFRICOM Headquarters in Stuttgart Germany. Of note, the J5 planners indicated that the East Africa Campaign plan would be complete in early 2012 for Joint Staff approval.

initiatives; the Africa Contingency Operations Training and Assistance (ACOTA) program and the Partnership for Regional East Africa Counterterrorism (PREACT).[11]

CJTF-HOA executes their missions in direct support of the Special Operations Command Africa (SOCAF); whose objectives are to build operational capacity, strengthen regional security, and implement effective communications strategies in support of AFRICOM's strategic objectives. These objectives include eradicating violent extremist networks such as Al Shabaab and their supporting networks through programs such as ACOTA and PREACT.[12] The special operations component of CJTF-HOA provides an invaluable resource that furthers USG efforts to combat terrorist groups and build partner nation CT capacity. A recent example is CJTF-HOA's support for Djibouti's efforts to train Somali TFG soldiers to assume a larger role in promoting security in the region. The 2010 QDR identified building security capacity in partner nations as one of the six key Department of Defense (DOD) mission areas.

The task force, although continuing to mature, is well established under a priority effort for AFRICOM, however a lack of CT prioritization for Somalia at both the national and combatant command level has allowed the Al Shabaab terrorist network to not only emerge, but flourish in the failed state. AFRICOM continues to emphasize persistent engagement with partner nations and partner capacity in order to promote regional

---

[11] The African Contingency Operations Training and Assistance (ACOTA) program, formerly the African Crisis Response Initiative (ACRI), is a United States program to train military trainers and equip African national militaries to conduct peace support operations and humanitarian relief.
The Partnership for Regional East African Counterterrorism (PREACT) is a U.S. funded and implemented multi-year, multi-faceted program designed to build the counterterrorism capacity and capability of member countries to thwart short-term terrorist threats and address longer-term vulnerabilities. PREACT member countries include Burundi, Comoros, Djibouti, Ethiopia, Kenya, Rwanda, Seychelles, Somalia, Sudan, Tanzania, and Uganda.

[12] *2011Posture Statement – United States Africa Command*, Statement of General Carter Ham, USA, Commander United States Africa Command to The House Armed Services Committee, April 5, 2011, 33.

security and stability and prevent conflict; however, as addressed previously, the indirect approach implemented by AFRICOM's main counterterrorism task force fails to produce results and the risk of a terrorist attack on the U.S. emanating from the AFRICOM area of responsibility continues to exist. As noted earlier in this chapter, General Ham expressed optimism that as SOF forces draw down in Iraq potential exists for a more focused SOF approach to Somalia. In Admiral McRaven's testimony to Congress before his confirmation as the Commander of the United States Special Operations Command (USSOCOM), he addressed two key issues on Somalia. He stated that USSOCOM would work in concert with AFRICOM's approach to building security capacity with partner nations on the continent and that SOF would support their mission to defeat transnational threats. He also indicted a potential peace dividend in ISR assets from the CENTCOM AOR that could be retasked to the Horn of Africa in support of CT efforts.[13]

AFRICOM Challenges

Building partnership capacity provides the foundation for many of AFRICOM's strategic objectives that are linked to defeating Al Shabaab and eliminating the safe haven that exists in Somalia. Over the past two years initiatives in capacity building and partner nation bilateral training such as ACOTA and PREACT are critical first steps in the U.S efforts. However, a holistic approach to Africa's problems and challenges is the best way to further U.S., international, and partner nation interests. The U.S. must

---

[13] U.S. Senate Committee on Armed Services, *Advance Policy Questions for VADM William H. McRaven to Admiral and Commander of US Special Operations Command*, Washington DC, June 2011, 18.

continue to support and facilitate a whole of nation approach to countering Al Shabaab in Somalia and seek and sustain regional partnerships to erode terrorist support and their support of legitimacy. However, as stated by General Ward, ─building regional stability and security will take many years of sustained and dedicated effort and there is no conspicuous finish line."[14] Therefore, enduring Congressional support is indispensable and will assist in AFRICOM's collective effort to prevent instability that leads to extremism, violence, and armed conflict, thereby better protecting U.S. interests and the American people.

---

[14] *2011Posture Statement – United States Africa Command*, Statement of General Carter Ham, USA, Commander United States Africa Command to The House Armed Services Committee, April 5, 2011, 35.

CHAPTER 6: CONCLUSION

"If you don't visit the bad neighborhoods...the bad neighborhoods are going to visit you." [1]

- Thomas Friedman

U.S. Security policy has been driven in the recent years by our counterterrorism efforts, which both the Bush and Obama Administrations identified as a top priority. The terrorists in Somalia can be defeated, but doing so presents an extraordinary challenge. A viable counterterrorism strategy must be implemented in Somalia where the terrorist threat is growing. There is no doubt that Somalia has become the ideal safe haven to grow, breed and export terrorism and it remains in the best interest of the United States to help rebuild the country. If the U.S. can accept its defeat in 1993 and learn from the mistakes it made, it has a real chance of making a difference in order to defeat this transnational terrorist threat. The lesson to be learnt is not to look the other way. [2]

To defeat Al Shabaab in Somalia, there are several steps that need to take place. First, we must deny Al Shabaab safe haven protection in Somalia. Somalia serves as a safe haven for three reasons: under development, incompetent governance, and disillusioned people. As observed in both Iraq and Afghanistan, successful military operations rooted out the terrorist insurgency networks from these regions resulting in the transnational movement to areas like Somalia which offered AQ the ability to train and coordinate attacks. In Iraq and Afghanistan, success was tied to large numbers of forces

---

[1] Thomas Friedman, New York Times Columnist following the 9/11 attacks, http://www.brainyquote.com/quotes/authors/t/thomas_friedman.html (accessed February 5, 2012).

[2] Jane's Terrorism and Insurgency Center, Somalia: Forgotton Terrorism Base, February 33, 2005. http://jtic.janes.com (accessed October 15, 2011).

occupying the countries. Currently, the final withdrawal of military forces from Iraq is underway and by the end of 2011 all forces will be out of Iraq. Simultaneously, the mission in Afghanistan is nearing the final phases after over a decade of costly fighting. Why is this important? The U.S. is not ready to embark on another counterinsurgency ground war with large numbers of U.S. military personnel on foreign soil which presents a challenge to the U.S. on the security situation in Somalia. The time may come where the U.S. will have to make a decision on a large scale troop deployment, but until that time arrives, the answer lies with the TFG and AMISOM.

The U.S. can undermine Al Shabaab's influence in the region through partnerships with the TFG and AMISOM. Denying the safe haven lies in protecting the people. The United States should address the U.N. Security Council to change the AMISOM mandate from peace keeping to peace enforcement which would allow AMISOM to conduct offensive operations directed against Al Shabaab. Mil-to-Mil initiatives originating out of CJTF-HOA such as the ACOTA and PREACT are critical first steps in strengthening AMISOM forces ability to be a viable force to face Al Shabaab and with time and resources will be effective. The next issue is troop numbers. As we saw in Iraq and Afghanistan, you must have a significant number of forces on the ground in the communities and towns to protect the people. Defeating Al Shabaab rests in protecting and securing the people.

The U.S. should work with the African Union to request an increase in numbers for the AMISON mission. The AMISOM commander estimated that he would need an increase in troop strength from 8,000 to approximately 20,000. The issue is finding these large numbers of troops. The U.N. should offer humanitarian and defense incentives to

African Union countries that support AMISOM as a way to gain support in the region. The U.S. should leverage partner nations under the CT umbrella to assist the TFG and AMISOM in developing a plan for providing logistical support, equipment, funding and counterinsurgency training for the TFG and AMISOM. Protecting the Somali people and training and resourcing the TFG and AMISOM forces are the first essential steps to denying Al Shabaab their safe haven. Each of these tasks is directly nested in our National Security Strategy on protecting the American people and our interests. The United States Africa Command can provide the means to accomplish training and resourcing tasks.

In conjunction with training and equipping AMISOM forces, the U.S. should build TFG governance capacity by training and providing recourses. Training the TFG in sound governance practices, combating terrorism and institution building is essential in building legitimacy to gain trust and confidence in the Somali people. U.S. policy should be focused on security and economic growth. Following successful operations by AMISOM and the TFG, a legitimate post-TFG government supported by the people is essential to the overall success of Somalia.

The East Africa region is currently the priority region for Africa Command and as General Ham, the Commander of AFRICOM, stated and he is hoping for a peace dividend from Iraq and Afghanistan in Special Operations Forces (SOF) who are inherently the most highly skilled and trained forces in foreign internal defense to accomplish these tasks though AFRICOM's CJTF-HOA mission in Djibouti. The special operations component of CJTF-HOA provides an invaluable resource that furthers USG efforts to combat terrorist groups and build partner nation CT capacity through mil-to-mil training. Admiral McRaven, the commander of the United States Special Operations Command who understands the importance of the region and the much needed success for both the TFG and AMISOM has pledged his support in personnel and equipment. Counterterrorism is an integral task completed by SOF forces and these assets are needed to disrupt the numerous Al Shabaab terrorist training camps in Somalia. These camps are the center of gravity for the terrorist threat emanating from Somalia that poses a threat to our homeland and its interests. These camps have been the focal point for U.S. citizens that have traveled to Somalia to become terrorist operatives for AQ. Through a SOF economy of force mission, these camps can be disrupted and dismantled through direct action missions similar to recent operations against high value targets like Saleh Nabhan in 2009. Disrupting these terrorist training camps can be accomplished by defeating the threat in the United States as well. When possible, kinetic operations should be subordinate to options that provide security for the Somali people, promote improved governance of the TFG or post TFG government and increase economic capacity.

Over that last decade, the majority of the United State's counterterrorism effort has been directed at preventing an attack by AQ on our homeland; however, the three recent terrorist attacks on our soil prove that this is a significant task. It is important to understand that the threat is not always in some distant land, but often right on our doorstep growing in our hometowns, communities and schools in the Somali diasporas. These diasporas are a source of recruits, logistics, and finances for Al Shabaab. We must focus our capabilities to build resilience within our communities here at home against AQ inspired radicalization, recruitment, and mobilization to violence. We must ensure that we remain engaged in the full range of community concerns and interests. We must support community leaders as they develop solutions tailored to their own particular circumstances as a critical part of our whole-of-government approach that contributes to our counterterrorism goals.

A successful counterterrorism strategy must address the nature of the threat and implement a systematic whole of government approach to defeat Al Shabaab and Al Qaeda in Somalia. Understanding the nature of this threat can lay out the foundation for a detailed strategy, help educate our senior political and military leaders and drive a reexamination of our U.S. policy on Somalia.

BIBLIOGRAPHY

2010 Posture Statement – United States Africa Command, Statement of General William E. Ward, USA, Commander United States Africa Command to The House Armed Services Committee, 9-10 March 2010.

2011Posture Statement – United States Africa Command, Statement of General Carter Ham, USA, Commander United States Africa Command to The House Armed Services Committee, April 5, 2011.

Al Shabab: Suicide Bomber in Somalia Was American, ABC News http://abcnews.go.com/Blotter/al-shabab-suicide-bomber-somalia-american/story?id=14851524, (accessed October 31, 2011).

AMISOM Bulletin, *Somalia is the Frontline in the Global Fight against Violent Extremism*, Issue 2, March 15, 2010, http://www.africa-union.org/root/au/auc/departments/psc/amisom/Bulletin/2010/AMISOM_%20BULLETIN_ISSUE%20NO%202.pdf (accessed September 13, 2011)

AMISOM: African Mission in Somalia, The African Union Commission, 2008, http://www.africa-union.org/root/au/auc/departments/psc/amisom/amisom.htm, (accessed September13, 2011).

Brainy Quotes, Quoted from Friedman, Thomas, http://www.brainyquote.com/quotes/authors/t/thomas_friedman.html, (accessed February 5, 2012).

Clausewitz, Carl Von, *On War*, (Random House, New York), 1993.

Committee on Foreign Relations, *Al Qaeda in Yemen and Somalia: A ticking Time Bomb*, A Report to the committee on Foreign Relations, 111th Congress, 2d Session, US Government Printing Office, January 21, 2010.

Dagne, Ted, *Somalia: Current Conditions and Prospects for a Lasting Peace*, Specialist in African Affairs, Congressional Research Service, August 31, 2011.

Director of National Intelligence Dennis C. Blair, Annual Threat Assessment of the U.S. Intelligence Community for the Senate Select Committee on Intelligence, February 2, 2010.

Fuller, J.F.C., The *Conduct of War*, (Da Capo Press, New Brunswick, New Jersey), 1992.

Gates, Robert M., *Quadrennial Defense Review Report*, Washington DC: Government Printing Office, February 2010.

Grace, Nick, The Long War Journal, Shabaab reaches out to Al Qaeda senior leaders, announces death al Sudani, September 2, 2008, http://www.longwarjournal.org/archives/2008/09/shabab_reaches_out_t.php (accessed Ocrober 7, 2011).

Grenade Attack in Kenya Follows Threats From Al Shabaab, Voice in America, October 24, 2011. http://www.voanews.com/english/news/africa/Grenade-Attack-Wounds-13-in-Kenya-132429548.html, (accessed October 24, 2011).

Horwitz, Jeffery H., *Pirate, Terrorists and Warloards* (New York: Skyhorse Publishing), 2009.

Harnisch, Christopher, The Terror Threat from Somalia: The internationalization of Al Shabaab, American Enterprise Institute, February 12, 2010.

Lawrence, T.E., *Revolt in the Desert* (George H. Doran Company), 1927.

Liban, Said, *U.S. Dual-Track Policy in Somalia*, November 24, 2010, http://www.worldpress.org/Africa/3657.cfm, (Accessed December 1, 2011).

Panetta, Leon, U.S. Secretary of Defense, *Panetta Warms of Retreat in Africa*, Washington Times, October 14, 2011.

Ploch, Lauren, *Africa Command: U.S. Strategic Interests and the Role of the U.S. Military in Africa*, Congressional Research Service - RL34003, July 22, 2011.

President George W. Bush, Speech to Congress, September 20, 2001, http://www.pearlharbor.org/speech-bush-sep-20-2001.asp (accessed October 16, 2011).

Losey, Brian L., *Conflict Prevention in East Africa – the Indirect Approach*, Prism, Center for Complex Operations, Vol. 2, No. 2. March 2011.

Naval Post Graduate School, *Radicalization Within the Somali-American Diaspora: Countering the homegrown Terrorist Threat*, Scott E. Mulligan, December 2009.

Quotes from the Movie *"Blackhawk Down,"* First Quotes, Major General William Garrison, Commander, Task Force Ranger. http://www.finestquotes.com/movie_quotes/movie/Black%20Hawk%20Down/page/0.htm (accessed February 5, 2012).

Remarks by Assistant to the President for Homeland Security and Counterterrorism John Brennan at CSIS, *Securing the Homeland by Renewing American Strength, Resilience and Values,* May 26, 2010, http://www.whitehouse.gov/the-press-office/remarks-assistant-president-homeland-security-and-counterterrorism-john-brennan-csi (accessed September 13, 2011).

Remarks by Honorable Michael E. Leiter, Director National Counterterrorism Center at the Aspen Institute, April 9, 2009, http://www.dni.gov/speeches/20090409_speech.pdf (accessed August 23, 2011).

Snyder, R., Operation *Restore Hope/Battle of Mogadishu*, History 135, August 2001, http://novaonline.nvcc.edu/eli/evans/his135/Events/Somalia93/Somalia93.html (accessed August 3, 2011).

Somalia Diaspora News, *FBI Confirms 1 Suicide Bomber in attack in Mogadishu was Minnesota Man*, June 9, 2011, http://somalidiasporanews.com/index.php/2011/06/fbi-confirms-1-suicide-bomber-in-last-weeks-attack-in-mogadishu-somalia-was-minnesota-man/ (accessed August 3, 2011).

Somalia: Current Situation, Somaliweyn, December 31, 2010, http://somaliweyn.somaliweyn.org/index.php?Itemid=9&catid=3:english-news&id=261:somalia-current-situation&option=com_content&view=article (accessed September 1, 2011).

Stephanie Hanson, *Somalia's Transitional Government*, Council on Foreign Relations May 12, 2008, http://www.cfr.org/somalia/somalias-transitional-government/p12475#p2 (accessed September 01, 2011).

Stephanie Hanson, Al-Shabaab, Council on Foreign Relations, August 10, 2011, http://www.cfr.org/somalia/al-shabaab/p18650 (accessed September 13, 2011).

Sun Tsu, *The Art of War*, Popular Quotes, http://www.artofwar.net/china/quotes.htm, (accessed February 5, 2012).

Szrom, Charlie, *Al Queda's Operating Environment – A New Approach to the War on Terror*, American Enterprise Institute, March 2011.

The changing Security Situation in Somalia: Implications for Humanitarian Action, The Brookings Institution, January 12, 2010, http://www.brookings.edu/~/media/Files/events/2010/0112_somalia/0112_somalia.pdf (accessed August 28, 2011).

The New York Times, *U.S. Relies on Contractors in Somalia Conflict*, August 10, 2011, http://www.nytimes.com/2011/08/11/world/africa/11somalia.html?pagewanted=all (accessed August 11, 2011).

The New York Times, White House Weighs Limits of Terror Fight, Charlie Savage, September 15, 2011. http://www.nytimes.com/2011/09/16/us/white-house-weighs-limits-of-terror-fight.html?pagewanted=all (accessed October 18, 2011).

The New York Times, Three Terrorists Groups in Africa pose Threat to the U.S., American Commander says. September 14, 2011.

http://www.nytimes.com/2011/09/15/world/africa/three-terrorist-groups-in-africa-pose-threat-to-us-general-ham-says.html, (accessed Novenber 2, 2011).

U.S. Department of Defense, Office of the Assistant Secretary of Defense (Public Affairs) Speech on U.S. Security Strategy for Sub-Saharan Africa, Published by the Office of International Security Affairs, Department of Defense, August 01, 1995.

U.S. Department of State, *Is Somalia Dangerous? US Policy in the Horn of Africa*, Eunice Reddick, Office Director of East African Affairs, October 4, 2006.

U.S. House of Representatives Committee on Homeland Security, Majority Investigative Report, *Al Shabaab: Recruitment and radicalization within the Muslim Community and the Threat to the Homeland*, Washington DC, July 27, 2011.

U.S. House of Representatives Resolution 1538 Condemning the July 11, 2010, terrorist attacks in Kampala, Uganda. 111th Congress, 2d Session, July 20, 2010.

U.S. President, *National Security Strategy*, Washington DC: Government Printing Office, May 2010.

U.S. President, *National Strategy for Counterterrorism*, Washington DC: Government Printing Office, June 2011.

U.S. President, *National Strategy for Homeland Security*, Homeland Security Council, Washington DC: Government Printing Office, October 2007.

U.S. Secretary of Defense, *National Defense Strategy*, Washington, DC: Government Printing Office, June 2008.

U.S. Secretary of Defense, *National Military Strategic Plan for the War on Terrorism*, Washington, DC: Government Printing Office, February 1, 2006.

Chairman of the Joint Chiefs of Staff, *The National Strategy of the United States of America,* Washington, DC: Government Printing Office, February 2011.

U.S. Senate Committee on Armed Services, *Advance Policy Questions for VADM William H. McRaven to Admiral and Commander of US Special Operations Command*, Washington DC, June 2011.

U.S. Senate Committee on Armed Services, *Nomination of VADM William H. McRaven to Admiral and Commander of US Special Operations Command*, Washington DC, June 28, 2011.

United States Government Accounting Office, *Improved Planning, Training, and Interagency Collaboration Could Strengthen DOD's Efforts in Africa*, Defense

Management, Report to the Subcommittee on National Security and Foreign Affairs on Oversight and Government Reform, House of Representative, GAO-10-794, July 2010.

─Young Somali Men Missing from Minneapolis," *USA Today*, November 27, 2008. http://www.usatoday.com/news/nation/2008-11-26-missing-somalis_N.htm (accessed September 14, 2011).